How To Submit And Distribute Apps On The Google Play Store:

Learn to generate a signed release APK file from the Android Studio, create a developer account, and publish your app on the Google Play Store

By
Joseph Correa

COPYRIGHT

This publication is designed to provide accurate and authoritative information in regard to the subject matter covered. It is sold with the understanding that neither the author nor the publisher is engaged in rendering advice. If technical assistance is needed, consult with an app specialist in the IT field that may address detailed issues. This book is considered a guide and should not be used in any way otherwise.

ACKNOWLEDGEMENTS

This book is dedicated to my family. Thank you for giving me the inspiration to make this book possible.

How To Submit And Distribute Apps On The Google Play Store:

Learn to generate a signed release APK file from the Android Studio, create a developer account, and publish your app on the Google Play Store

By
Joseph Correa

TABLE OF CONTENTS

INTRODUCTION

This book will teach you how to successfully submit an app to the Google Play Store and get it approved using a step by step process from start to finish. Learn how to open a developer account and become a registered Google® developer. You will learn how to generate a signed release APK file from the Android Studio, create a developer account, and publish your app on the Google Play Store.

Common mistakes are addressed and solutions to these mistakes are detailed to help you over come frustrating situations that might be easily fixed and corrected to get you through the app submission process successfully.

A step by step process will be explained in each chapter like this:

Chapter One: The Google Play Store

Chapter Two: How to Generate a signed release APK file from the Android studio

Chapter Three: Create a Google Play Developer account

Chapter Four: Publish your app on the Google Play Store

Chapter Five: Common mistakes in Google App distribution and how to avoid it

CHAPTER ONE

The Google Play Store

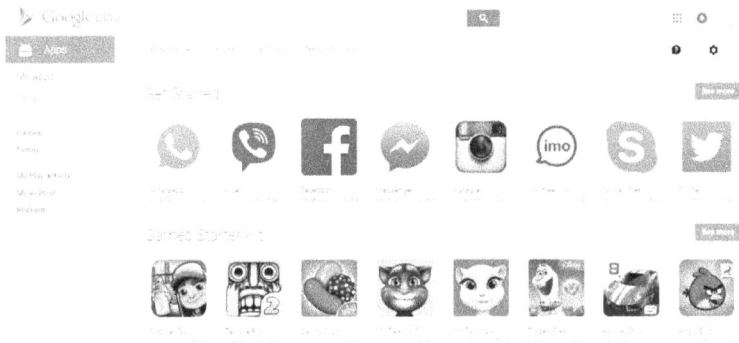

The beauty of being an app developer in this era is the sheer range and variety of platforms, tools and environments you can develop with and for. It is not an overstatement to say that there are many choices nowadays, but, nowhere does this hold truer than developing for the Android platform.

The Google play store is the easiest way to distribute your Android app. Although, it is not the only way, but, it is the easiest way to reach millions of potential users. Publishing your first app is not as difficult as you think, with a few steps highlighted in this e-book, you will be able to have your app ready for download in next to no time. But before we do that, let's take a look at the reasons why you need to publish your app on Google Play store.

Why distribute your app on Google Play

Google Play store is the first ranking store for distributing Android apps. Publishing your apps on Google play means you are exposing it to more than a billion active Android users in more than 190 countries around the world.

Android smartphone and tablet users are also growing rapidly. It is forecasted to continue growing worldwide. This means that your app will continue to have large markets on the Google play store.

More than a billion apps have been downloaded on Google play. So, you can be rest assured that your app will not sit on the shelf.

Prerequisite for publishing apps on Google play

Before you publish your apps on Google play and distribute them to others, you need to get your apps ready. The following points below will help you to get set.

1.   Read Google Play policies and agreements

Make sure you read and understand the Google play program policies before you register. Google play imposes the policies and if you violate it, your apps will be suspended. If you continue to violate it, your developer's account will be terminated.

2.   Test your app for quality

Before you publish your apps on Google play store, you need to make sure that they meet the basic quality required for all Android apps for all the devices you are planning to target. You can check the quality of your apps by setting up a test environment and testing it against a set of quality criteria that goes for all Android apps. You can check the guidelines here -

http://developer.android.com/distribute/essentials/quality/core.html

3.   Know your app's content rating

Google play wants all Android users to set a content rating for their apps. This will enable Google play users to know its maturity level. Choose the appropriate rating for your app before you publish it. Below are available content rating levels:

a.   Everyone
b.   Low maturity
c.   Medium maturity
d.   High maturity

Android users can set their desired maturity level for browsing on their devices. Google play filters apps based on that setting, so the content rating you choose can affect the app's distribution to users.

4. Know your country distribution

Google play allows you to control the countries and territories you want to distribute your apps to. In order to reach a larger customer base, it is advisable for you to distribute your apps to all available countries and territories. However, you can also exclude one or two countries from your distribution.

You need to know your country of distribution from the onset, because it can affect time zone support, local pricing, legal requirements etc.

5. Check the size of your app

Google play specifies the maximum size for an APK file published on the Google play to be 50mb. If your app is more than that size, you will want to offer a secondary download (APK expansion files). You can upload two files of about 2GB in size for each APK using the APK expansion files.

6. Check your app's platform and screen compatibility ranges

Before you publish your app, it is important to ensure that your app is designed to run properly on the Android platform versions and on the device screen sizes that you plan to target. The app compatibility is defined by API level. You need to check that the minimum version your app is compatible with <minSdkVersion> as it will affect the distribution to all other Android devices once you publish it.

You should ensure that your app looks great on different screen sizes and pixel densities you want to support. You can follow the advice here - http://developer.android.com/guide/practices/screens_support.html

7.   Decide whether your app will be free or paid

You can publish and distribute your apps on Google Play as a free download or paid. Free apps can be accessed and downloaded by any user in Google play. However, paid apps can only be downloaded by users who are in a country that support paid downloads and have an account on Google play with their payment method specified, such as a credit card or direct carrier billing. Knowing whether you want to publish your app as free or paid is very important, because once you set it as a free app, it must remain free, you cannot change it. But, if you want to change your paid app to free it is possible, however, you cannot revert it back to paid again.

Required tools

Required tools / Resources

1.   The app

2.   The APK file

3.   US $25 registration fee

4.   A browser

5.   Internet connection

6.   A computer

CHAPTER TWO

How to Generate a signed release APK file from the Android studio

Once you have finished developing your android application and tested it, the next step is to prepare it for submission to the Google Play store. Before you submit the app, you must package it for release by compiling it in release mode and sign it with a private key that shows you are the application's developer. In this stage, you will learn how to get the private key and prepare your app for release.

Change the build variant for the app

The first step is for you to change the build variant for the app from debug to release.

You can access the build variants tool from the window quick access menu by the right hand corner of the Android studio main window as shown below.

Terminal

Event Log

Favorites

Build Variants

Gradle Console

Messages

Android

Gradle

TODO

Structure

Maven Projects

Commander

Project

: Android   Q: Messages

Gradle build finished with 2 warnings(s) in 12 sec

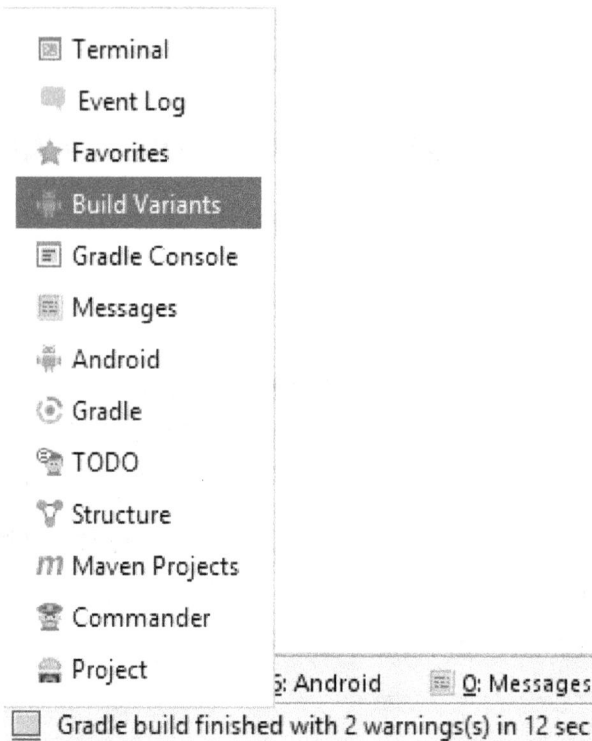

Once you see the build variants tool window, click on it and change the Build variant settings for all the modules listed from debug to release.

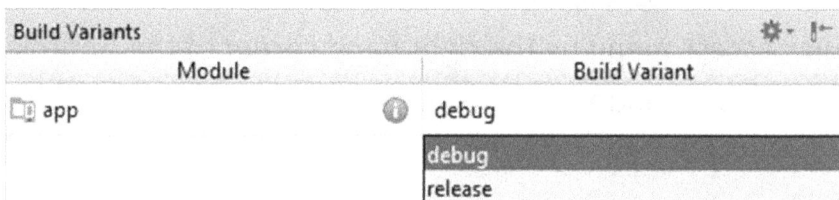

Build Variants	
Module	Build Variant
app	debug
	debug
	release

When you are through with that, the project is configured to build in release mode. The next thing is to configure the signing key information. You will use it when generating the signed application package.

Create a Keystore file

Here, you will create a keystore file. To do this, Click on **Build**, then **generate signed APK**. Below is the picture showing the Generate signed APK wizard dialog box.

If you have a release keystore file, click on "**Choosing existing**" button and select the appropriate file. If you don't have a keystore file, click on "**create new...**" button to show the New Key store dialog box.

Generate a private Key

Click on the button on the right of Keystore path field and enter a name for the keystore file.

The next thing you will do now is to generate a new private key with which you will use to sign in to the application package.

Now, put in your "**password**" with which you will protect the keystore file.

*   Enter an **"alias"** to reference your key. It can be characters.
*   Put in a strong "**password**" to protect the key.
*   Specify the number of years for the "**validity**" of the key. Google recommends a duration of 27 years.

Fill in your first and last name, Organizational unit, organization, city or locality, state or province and your country code.

When you finish, click on **"ok"** to move to the package creation.

Create the application APK file

The next thing is to generate your APK file. You will have to generate the APK package in release mode and sign in with your newly created private key. You will see the APK file dialog box as shown below.

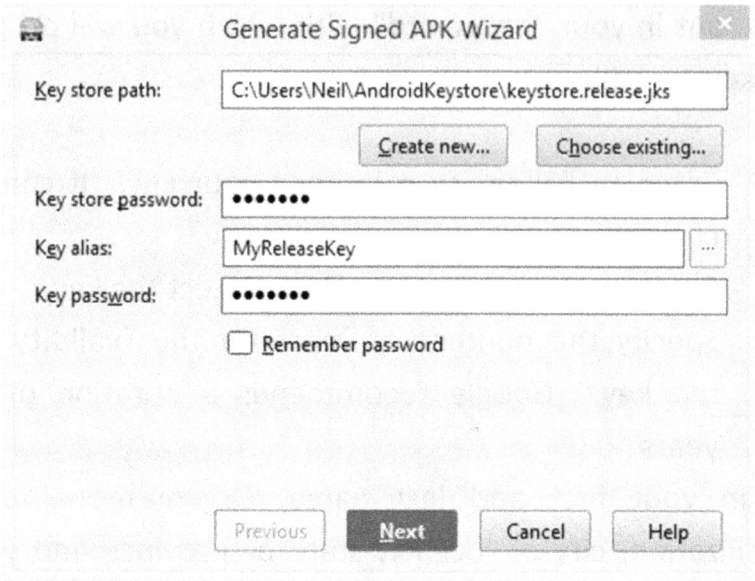

Check to ensure that the settings are correct, then click on **"next"** button to generate the APK file.

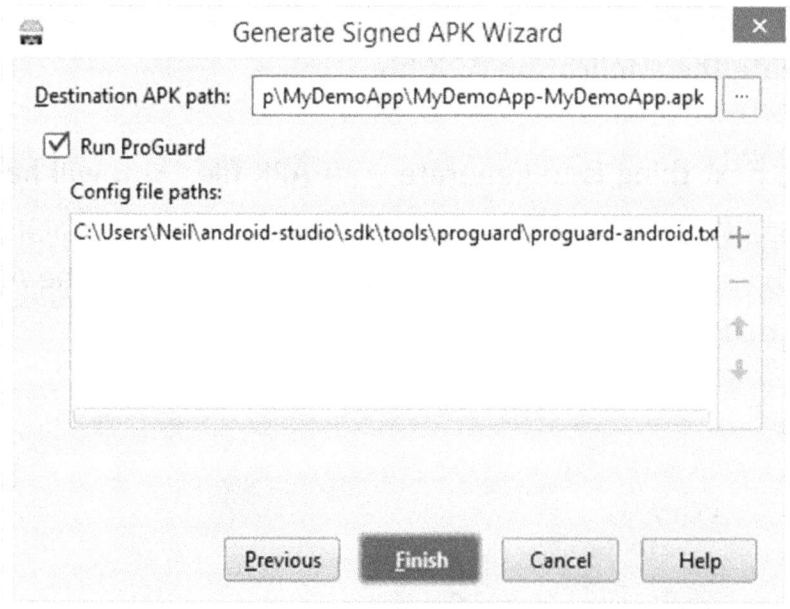

In the screen displayed (shown above), you will see the destination APK setting. The setting needs you to confirm or verify that the location into which the APK file is generated is acceptable by you. If you want to change the location, click on the button on the right and specify a different location for it.

Check the "**Run proGuard**" box. This feature performs a series of optimization and verification tasks that can lead to smaller and efficient byte code. Click the "**finish**" button. The Gradle system will compile the application in release mode for you. Once you finish the building, a dialog box will show up, giving you the option to open the folder containing the APK file in an explorer window.

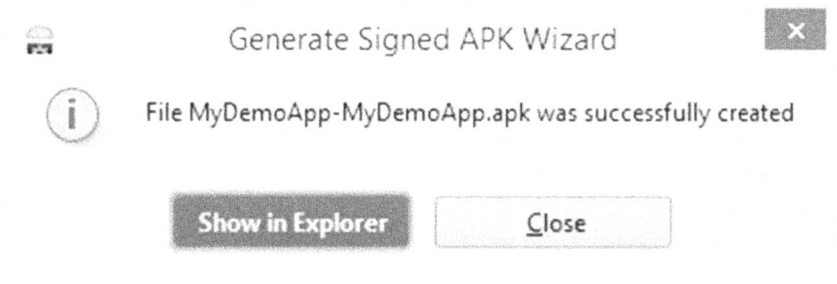

Generate Signed APK Wizard ☒

File MyDemoApp-MyDemoApp.apk was successfully created

Show in Explorer   Close

Your application is now ready to be submitted to the Google play store.

CHAPTER THREE

Create a Google Play Developer account

Now that your app and APK file is ready for distribution, it is time to upload it to the Google Play store. However, before you can do that, you will need to create a Google developer account. So, in this chapter, you will learn how to create a Google play developer account.

Creating a developer account

The first thing you need to create a developer account is a Google account. If you don't have one, you can create a new gmail account. Even if you have an existing account, it is recommended that you use a separate Google account for your app development activities.

Registering to develop and publish Android apps on the Google play store is not free. It comes with a price tag of $25. It is a one time fee and it is cheaper than registering as an Apple iOS developer platform.

To register for a Google Play developer account:

1.   Click on this URL Google Play Developer Console.

2.   Click on "create an account" to get a new Google account for your android developer activities.

3.   Fill in the form with the following details:

- First / Last Name
- Username (I.e. your proposed e-mail address). Choose a name that reflects your business/organisation appropriately.
- Password
- Confirm password
- Birthday
- Gender
- Mobile Phone
- Current e-mail address
- Captcha (To make sure you are human, enter the number displayed on the screen)
- Location
- Agreement to the Terms of Service and Privacy Policy (Read these carefully to make sure you understand what you are entering into)

You will be taken to another screen where you can:

- Choose to use a different Google Account for your Developer Console
- Accept the Google Play Developer distribution agreement (It is recommended that you read the agreement before you accept it - as with all agreements you might choose to enter into)
- Pay the registration fees
- Complete your account details

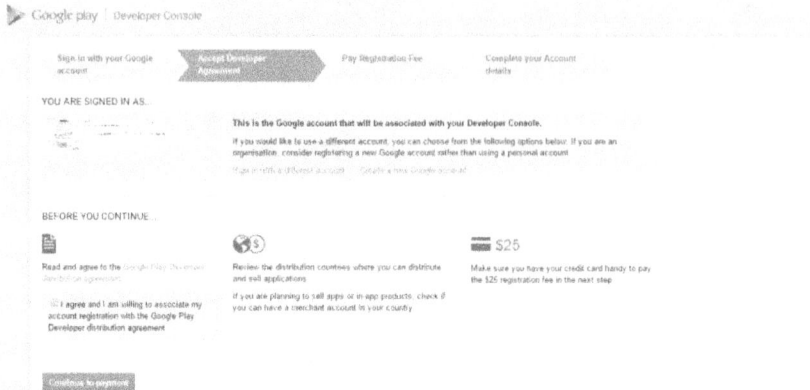

Click on "**Google play developer distribution agreement**". Once you read the Google Play Developer distribution agreement, and you are happy to enter into agreement to use the service, go back to the console dashboard and check the box.

Google Play Developer Distribution Agreement

Last modified: May 5, 2015 (view archived version)

Definitions

Authorized Carrier: A mobile network operator who is authorized to receive a distribution fee for Products that are sold to users of Devices on its network

Brand Features: the trade names, trademarks, service marks, logos, domain names, and other distinctive brand features of each party, respectively, as owned (or licensed) by such party from time to time.

Developer or You: Any person or company who is registered and approved by the Store to distribute Products in accordance with the terms of this Agreement

Developer Account: A publishing account issued to Developers that enables the distribution of Products via the Store

Developer Console: The console or other online tool provided by Google to developers to manage the distribution of Products and related administrative functions

Device: Any device that can access the Store, as defined herein

Google: Google Inc., a Delaware corporation with principal place of business at 1600 Amphitheatre Parkway, Mountain View, CA 94043, United States; Google Ireland Limited, a company incorporated in Ireland with principal place of business at Gordon House, Barrow Street, Dublin 4, Ireland; Google Commerce Limited, a company incorporated in Ireland with principal place of business at Gordon House, Barrow Street, Dublin 4, Ireland; and Google Asia Pacific Pte. Limited, a company incorporated in Singapore with principal place of business at 8 Marina View, Asia Square 1 #30-01, Singapore 018960.

Payment Account: A financial account issued by a Payment Processor to a Developer that authorizes the Payment Processor to collect and remit payments on the Developer's behalf for Products sold via the Store. Developers must be approved by a Payment Processor for a Payment Account and maintain their account in good standing to charge for Products distributed in the Store

Payment Processor(s): As specified and designated in the Developer Program Policies, a party authorized by Google to provide services that enable Developers with Payment Accounts to charge users for Products distributed via the Store.

Products: Software, content and digital materials distributed via the Store

BEFORE YOU CONTINUE...

Read and agree to the Google Play Developer Distribution Agreement

☐ I agree and I am willing to associate my account registration with the Google Play Developer distribution agreement

Review the distribution countries where you can distribute and sell applications

If you are planning to sell apps or in-app products, check if you can have a merchant account in your country

$25

Make sure you have your credit card handy to pay the $25 registration fee in the next step.

Continue to payment

Click on "**continue to payment**" to proceed to the next screen to enter your card details for the registration fee. Fill in the following details:

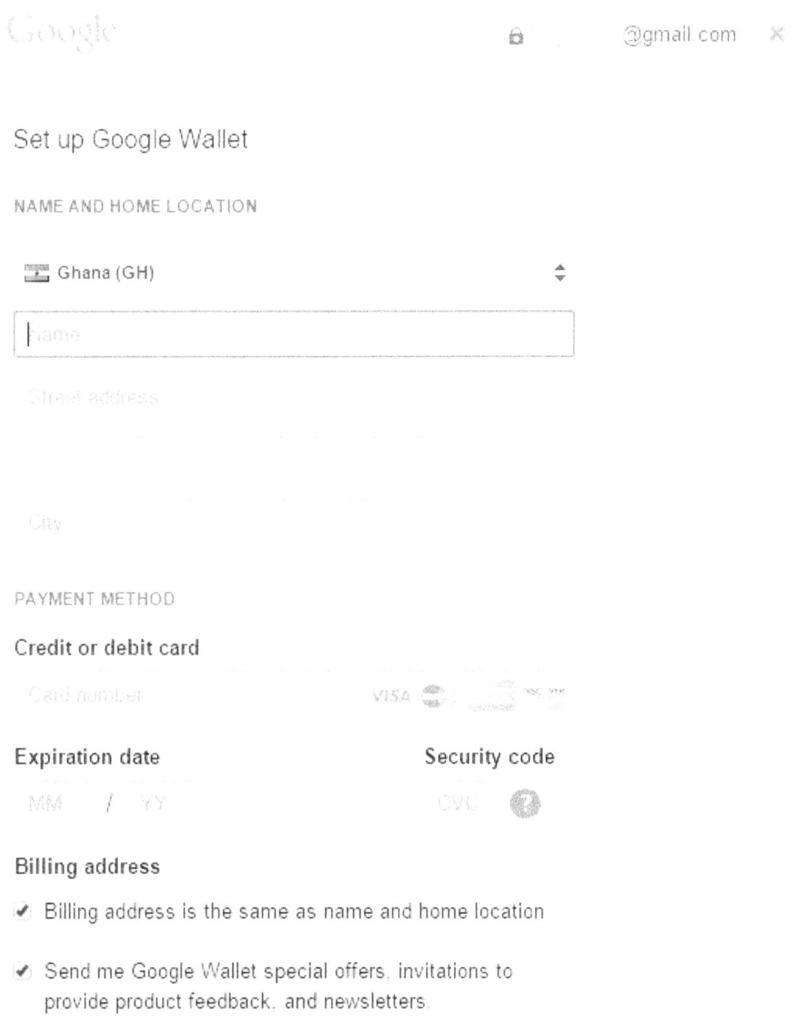

Google   🔒   @gmail.com   ✕

Set up Google Wallet

NAME AND HOME LOCATION

☰ Ghana (GH)   ⇕

Name

Street address

City

PAYMENT METHOD

Credit or debit card

Card number   VISA 💳

Expiration date   Security code

MM   /   YY   CVC ❓

Billing address

✔ Billing address is the same as name and home location

✔ Send me Google Wallet special offers, invitations to
  provide product feedback, and newsletters

I agree to the Google Payments Terms of Service and Privacy Notice.

Cancel **Accept and continue**

* Name
* Location
* Street address
* City
* Payment method (specify your payment method by selecting an option from the list of payment methods displayed)
* Fill your card expiration date and the security code
* Confirm if your billing address is the same as name and home location
* Specify if you want Google wallet special offers sent to your email address.

Read the terms of service. Be sure to read through the Google Wallet Buyer Terms and Conditions of use

Terms of Service - Buyer

August 5, 2013

This Terms of Service forms a legal agreement between you and Google Payment Corp. a wholly-owned subsidiary of Google Inc. ("Google"), which governs your access to and use of Google Wallet as a purchaser of merchandise, goods, or services. Please review this entire Terms of Service before you decide whether to accept it and continue with the registration process.

BY CLICKING ON THE "AGREE AND CONTINUE" BUTTON ON THE REGISTRATION PAGE, YOU AGREE TO BE BOUND BY THIS TERMS OF SERVICE.

1. Certain Defined Terms

The following defined terms appear in this Terms of Service.

- "You", "you" or "Buyer": A Customer that applies to, or registers to use, or uses, the Service to make Payment Transactions.
- Carrier Billing: Where offered to you, the payment process whereby GPC, on behalf of Seller, submits a Payment Transaction to the Carrier for billing to the Buyer's Carrier Billing Account.
- Carrier: A mobile telephone operator approved by GPC that offers a Carrier Billing Account.
- Carrier Billing Account: The monthly or other periodic billing account provided to you by your Carrier that you

Close

Click on "accept and continue"

You will need to check your information to make sure it is correct before you move to the next step. The fee is quoted in US Dollars (this will reflect on your credit card if the transaction is successful):

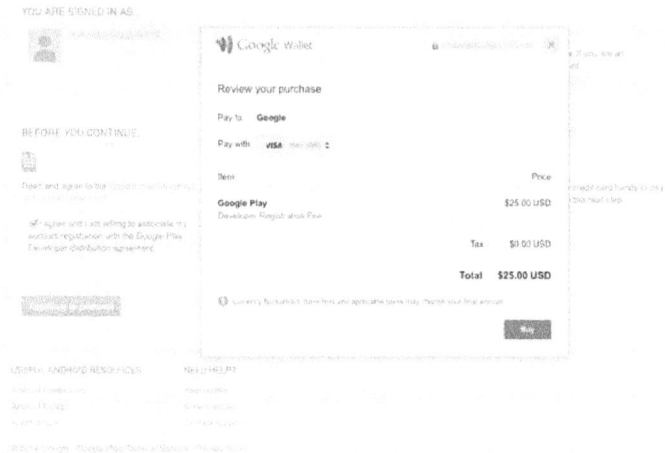

If the details shown in the confirmation screen are correct, click the "**Buy**" button. You can complete the rest of your registration as your payment is being processed.

The next thing is to complete your registration details

by filling in the following information:

- Developer Name (Ensure that the name you use is unique. It will be shown on the Google Play store under the name of your App. If you work for an organisation it will be good to use the organisation's name)
- Email Address
- Website
- Phone Number
- If you wish to receive Email updates from Google Play, you can check the box.

Once you've entered the necessary details into the form, click on "**Complete registration**" button.

Congratulations! You now have a Google play developer account.

CHAPTER FOUR

Publish your app on the Google Play Store

With your newly created Google developer account, you can proceed to publish your app on the store.

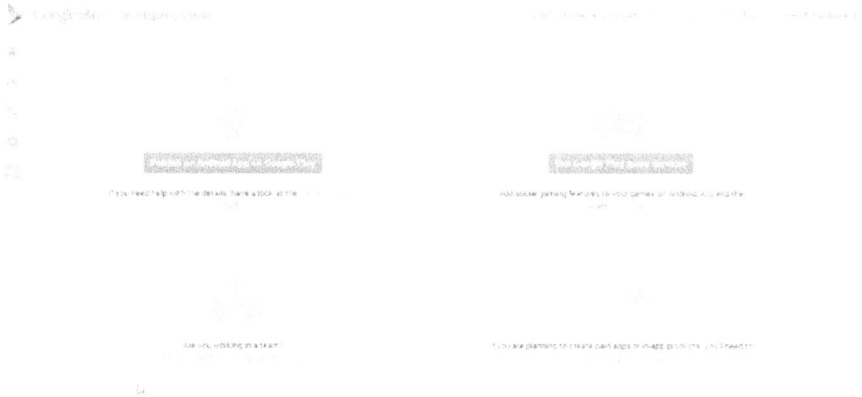

Click on "**Publish an Android app on Google Play**"

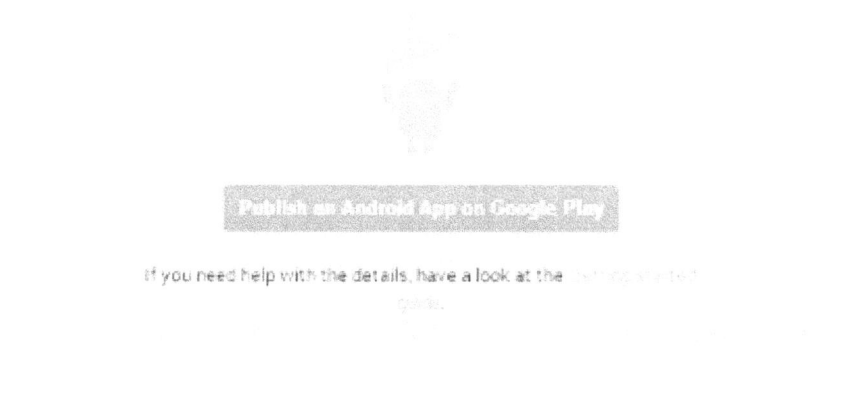

It is time to upload your APK file generated in Chapter One.

ADD NEW APPLICATION

Default language

English (United States) – en-US

Title

0 of 30 characters

What would you like to start with?

Upload APK   Prepare Store Listing   Cancel

Type in the title of your app and click on "**Upload APK**". You have a choice of whether you want to upload an APK file or prepare a store listing or cancel adding a new application.

NEW PLAIN OL' NOTES

APK

PRODUCTION

License keys are now managed for each application individually.

You can choose to upload the signed APK file that you generated or get a license key:

There is a need to prevent unauthorized distribution of your App, so click on the "**Get license key**" button where you can obtain a license key (which is automatically generated on your behalf) which you can then include in the APK binary.

Once you've included your license key, you can return to the APK screen.

Click on the "**Upload your first APK**" button which will load a modal window where you can choose to upload the signed APK file.

UPLOAD APK

Drop your APK file here, or select a file.

Browse files

Cancel

You can either drag your APK file into the box or hit browse to pick it up from your computer.

After you are done with the APK file uploading, you can click on "**store listing**" on the left hand side of the dashboard. This is where you will fill in all the information about your App that other users can see when they browse the App store.

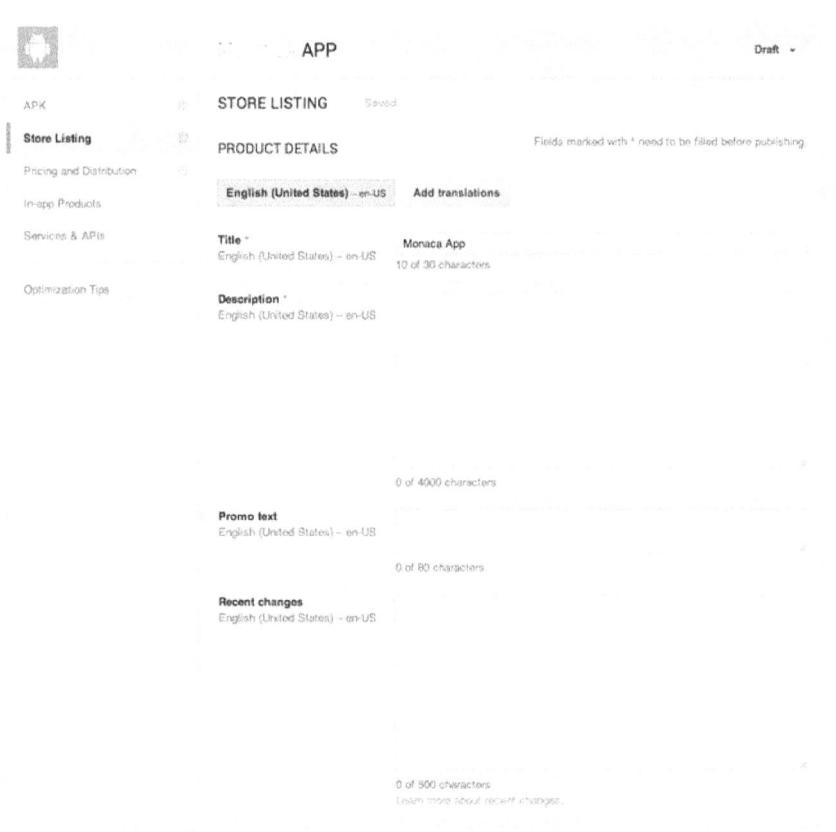

Fill in the following information:

Add Translation button

You can click on this button if you plan to distribute your app to users who speak other languages apart from English.

You can submit the translations of the app title and description. Google play will display it according to user's location.

Title:
This is the name of your app. Select a unique title to distinguish it from the numerous app in Google play store.

Description:
This is the description of what your app is all about. It can be up to 4000 characters.

Promo text
This is the text that accompanies your promotional pictures in a featured spot in Google play store.

Recent changes
This feature is used to let users know about the changes you make to your app.

Screenshots
These are the images of your app. Google play requires you upload your screenshots (it can be up to 8).

Application type
Choose the application type for your app. There are only two major application types in the Google play store -

Applications and Games. So choose the appropriate one that represents your app.

Category

Choose the category that fits your app.

Content rating

Select the appropriate content rating of your app.

Contact details

You must provide your contact details for support. It can be your website address, email or phone. Users can see it from the Google play store.

When you have finished filling out the store listing page, click on "**pricing and distribution**". This is where you will choose which country you want your app to be sold or distributed.

This is where you will also set the price for your app.

When you are done with the form, you will notice a drop down menu located in top right hand corner of the page. It will change from "Draft" to "**ready to publish**". Click the drop down menu and click on **"Publish this app"**.

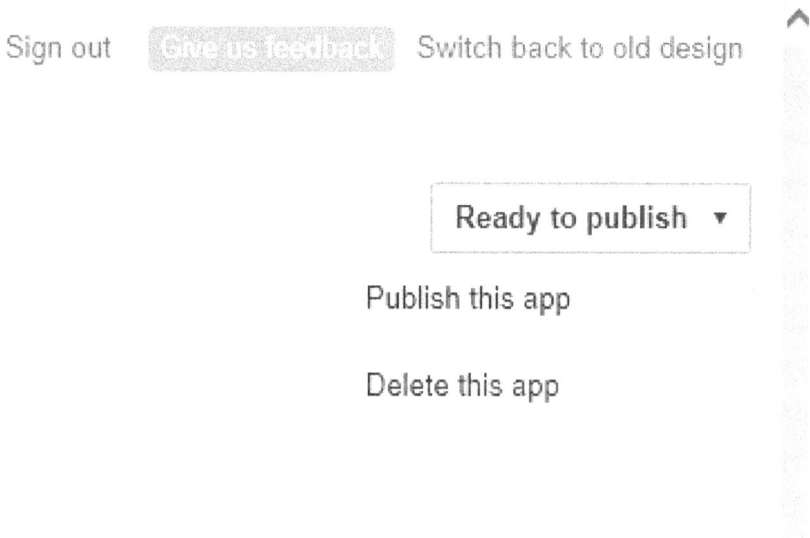

Sign out   Give us feedback   Switch back to old design

Ready to publish ▼

Publish this app

Delete this app

This may take a few hours or more, but eventually you'll be able to see your App available for other users of the Google Play store to download and install.

And that is how simple it is to distribute your Android Apps through the Google Play store as a registered developer.

CHAPTER FIVE

Common mistakes in Google App distribution and how to avoid it

Using other people's trademarked names

Google play policies explicitly mentioned that a developer should not impersonate other products or companies. You cannot use another person's trademark name. For example, you cannot use "Googlemusic browser" as the name of your app. It looks as if you are not impersonating Google. But it is not that simple and it is not too complicated either. If you must use a trademarked name, it is best you use them at the end of your app's title and add "for" to it. I.e. "Browser for Googlemusic". It shows that the app is not endorsed by Googlesmusic. Apart from that, you should also add the necessary attribution in your description. For instance, you can write - Googlemusic is a trademark of Google Inc. Most companies often offer guidelines on how to use their brand name appropriately. It will do you good to check their website first.

Also, you cannot modify a trademark name. For instance, you cannot use "Facebook ++".

Screenshots and other assets

You cannot use screenshots of copyrighted covers. Instead of doing that, you can create original images of your apps or use open content when taking the screenshots. The same thing applies to assets in your app.

Keyword spam

Using too many keywords in your app's description is referred to as spamming on Google play store. Instead of writing lots of keywords, write a few sentences explaining the function your apps. Make sure that you use related keywords. Unrelated keywords is also termed as spam.

Taking payment/donations from external sources

You are not allowed to use external payment methods except Google wallet. This is done through In-App purchases or different paid keys or donation apps. Other payment methods are used for products that can be used outside the app, such as, books. If you plan to use external methods of payment, you can only do that on your website.

Advertisements

Do not serve ads through the notification system or add home shortcuts or bookmarks for advertising purposes. Most users don't like it. You also need to separate your ads from your content. This will enable the ads to be seen at the bottom of your app. This will also enable your users to notice the ads, instead of confusing them with actual content or risk clicking them by mistake.

Again, showing ads outside your app is not allowed. This includes showing ads after users exit the application.

Icons

It is prohibited for you to use another product or company's icon, unless you ask for permission. For instance, you can use and modify the Android robot under specific terms (it is licensed under the creative commons attribution 3.0 license).

If you are not sure, you can produce your own icon or use open content. You can search for icons on Flaticon. It is a great resource and it is easy to search for icons on the platform. However, you need to provide credit for the CC icons.

Conclusion

You can see from the steps above that It is easy to publish your app on the Google play store. Hundreds of apps are submitted on a daily basis due to the demand for apps. Follow the steps detailed above and stay within the rules and guidelines specified by the app store so that you have no surprises. What are you waiting for? Get your apps out there and start making money today.